WALKING

ON THE

YORKSHIRE COAST

by

J. Brian Beadle

INTRODUCTION

Walking on Yorkshire's coastal paths can be a dangerous pastime for the un-wary. Please be extra vigilant whilst walking these paths, especially if you have children or animals with you. Some of the paths can be slippery when wet, some may have fallen into the sea after a winter storm whilst others may be well cared for by voluntary organisations. An offshore wind blowing at 10 m.p.h. when you leave home is probably building up to nearer 20 m.p.h. as it races out into the open sea from the cliff top. When walking on the beach have respect for the tide, it is so easy to be cut off. Please take care, go well prepared taking with you warm waterproof cloth-ing, food, water and the old favourites, map, compass and whistle.

Some of the walks have a strong historical theme to them. The old smugglers haunts can be fascinating. Try imagining what it would be like dodging the ex-cise man on a moonless night along the Bolts at Scarborough or Robin Hoods Bay, with a barrel of Brandy on your shoulder.

Picture the scene at Ravenscar when the flat bottomed ships edged their way onto the beach with a stinking cargo of urine for the Alum works. Then the sweating and toiling of men who were needed to haul it up the cliff. There was much mining activity along this part of the coast extracting clay, shale and jet.

Today, activity is in the leisure trade as walkers and cyclists explore the old paths along the coast. Before setting out on any of these routes I recommend that you consult the appropriate Ordnance Survey map for detail. The maps in the book are only a guide to the rights of way.

I'm sure you will enjoy walking along the coast of North Yorkshire.

J. Brian Beadle

1994

ISBN189900405
Revised and updated by C Armstrong 2011

INDEX

ROUTE 1

OLD STAITHES

Staithes is situated in a deep, rugged ravine 10 miles north west of Whitby. The main industry at Staithes is fishing. Many years ago fish that was to be cured was cut up & salted, brined, then laid out on the beach to dry. In the early nine-teenth century fifteen cobbles would have been engaged in the Herring industry. There were around 400 men and boys engaged in the fishing industry at Staithes.

Runswick Bay is a very scenic place. There are caves where the sea has washed holes in the rock. Like Staithes, fishing is prominent but perhaps is now surpassed by the leisure industry.

FACT FILE

Distance -7 miles (11km
Time -3 hours
Grading -Easy
Map -OS Landranger 101
Start -Runswick Bay. GR 807162.
Parking -Large car park at Runswick Bay.
Refreshments -Runswick Bay & Staithes. The Fox & Hounds at Dalehouse.

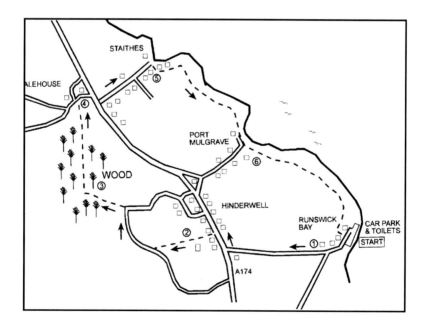

THE ROUTE

1.Start from the cliff top car park at Runswick Bay. Do not go down the hill into the old village it is better to park at the top and walk down later. Leave the park and take the road left to Hinderwell. Rejoin the A 174 at the war memorial in Hinderwell. Bear right into the village, then in about 50 yards cross the road and walk along a lane between house numbers 98 & 100. Continue along past the school to a stile.

2. Follow the track across the field then exit right onto a sometimes muddy lane. Follow the lane until it bends back towards the village. Do not follow the lane to the village but take the stile on the left into a field. Crossing the field brings you to another stile to take you downhill into a wood and a stream. Cross the footbridge and take the path uphill into a field and turn right.

3.Walk along the side of the field and at the corner of the field turn right into the wood. Be careful not to miss this turn! In the wood take the path to the left. Keep on this path for some time as it winds its way through the wood until you reach a junction of tracks. Go straight ahead here onto a wider path passing the sign for the Oak Ridge Nature Reserve. Continue on for a short while to a gate leaving the wood. Eventually down a steep hill to another gate into a caravan site.

4.Continue through the caravan site turning right over a wooden bridge, finally taking the dirt road on the left to take you to Dalehouse. At Dalehouse turn right past the Fox & Hounds to exit onto the A174. Go right for a few yards then cross the road to turn left to walk to Staithes old village.

5.Down the steep hill now into another world, the old houses and shops that haven't changed in a hundred years. Continue along through quaint old streets to the harbour where you will find the Cod & Lobster pub. Turn right along Church Street here to ascend the cobbled road and then steps to take you to the cliff top.

6.Follow the Cleveland Way signs to the left then an obvious path all the way along the cliffs to Port Mulgrave. Take to the road here for a short while then when it bends to the right, rejoin the cliff path to the left past some large boulders. Continue along the cliff until you see a sign pointing inland for Runswick Bay. Turn right here and follow the path to the road then left to the car park.

There are fine viewpoints along the cliffs between Runswick Bay and Staithes. To the north is the Boulby potash mine which reaches out under the sea and is the deepest mine in the country. The cliffs at Boulby are the highest cliffs in England and are a stimulating site from any angle. from any angle.

ROUTE 2

MULGRAVE WOODS

This walk through Mulgrave Woods is steeped in history and folklore. The focal point of the walk, the old castle, was probably built in Saxon times and is a crumbling but proud monument to its former glory. There have been three castles in the woods at Mulgrave. The Marquis of Normanby lives in today's castle which was built in the 18th century. But apart from the one which you are to visit there was another Mulgrave Castle built on an adjacent ridge by a Saxon Duke called Wada. Or was it the giant Wade who is said to have roamed these parts hundreds of years ago? My vote goes to the Saxon, but the giants tales are entertaining and add a flavour to the walk. Wada's castle would have been made from wood and only the Motte remains. It is on the adjacent ridge to the walk but is accessible from the Lythe -Ugthorpe road.

Mulgrave Castle is believed to have been built by the powerful family of Mauley and it was supposedly founded in Saxon times. In 1773 it was occupied by one Captain Phipps who led an expedition to the North Pole. Today, the ruins stand proud, if a little frail.

FACT FILE.

Distance -3½miles (6km)

Time -1½hours

Grading -Easy

Map -OS Landranger 94

Start -Sandsend. GR 239720

Refreshments -Sandsend

THE ROUTE

1.The walk starts in the village of Sandsend. There is ample parking on the road. Alternatively there is a small car park at the entrance to Mulgrave Woods. When approaching from Whitby enter Sandsend carefully, for where the road turns sharply over a narrow bridge you must turn s

2.The woods are only open on Wednesdays, Saturdays and Sundays, and not at all during the month of May. Enter the woods through the gate at the rear of the car park. Follow the path by the river side until it reaches the sawmill. Go through the mill yard and exit through a gate close to the bungalow on the right.

3.The woods have a mixture of deciduous and evergreen trees with a generous sprinkling of wild flowers in the undergrowth. When the path splits bear right. In fact keep bearing right each time there is a choice of route, except at the tunnel. Do not take the tunnel path at this stage. Eventually the path makes a rising 'U-turn' to the right. The path now becomes a little more over-grown and muddy underfoot but you are almost at the entrance to the castle.

4.At the top of the rise the overgrown stone walls of the early Mulgrave Castle loom into view, an impressive sight! Please read the notices on entering the Castle grounds as the structure of the walls are rather precarious. The huge mullioned window is still intact. What a magnificent place this must have been!.

5.Keep the Castle ruins on the right to exit at the diagonally opposite corner to which you arrived and drop down onto a path, turning left. At the clearing keep right.

6.This path eventually joins the one you came on and takes you back to the car park at Sandsend.

If you have time to spare on the way back you will find plenty of other paths to ramble about on and you may now explore through the tunnel! But do not venture too far or you will reach the new Mulgrave Castle which is the seat of the Marquis of Normanby.

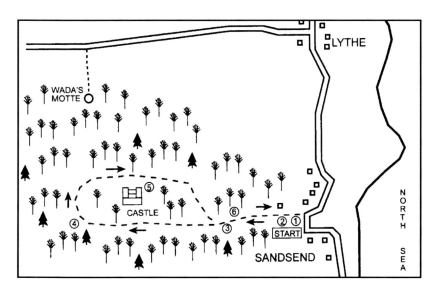

ROUTE 3
SEARCHING FOR A KIPPER!

No walking book on the east coast would be complete without a visit to Whitby and the consuming of one or more pairs of Fortune's oak smoked kippers! Where is Fortune's? On Henrietta Street. Where is Henrietta Street? Well, by the time that you visit it could well be in the harbour! The cliff is being undermined in the area and at the far end of the street serious erosion has taken place although restoration work is now in place giving access to the far pier again. I have titled this walk 'Searching for a Kipper' but it could easily have been called 'Looking for a Fortune'!

FACT FILE.

Distance -3 miles (5km)
Time -2½ hours (Plus finding the Kipper time)
Grading -Easy
Map -A Street Map of Whitby available from the Tourist Information Centre (Opposite the railway station.)
Start - Whitby Abbey car park GR905113.
Refreshments - No visit to Whitby would be complete without some locally caught fish and chips from one of the excellent shops around town. A visit to Botham's in Skinner Street would

Approach the Abbey car park from the A171 Scarborough to Whitby road. Now would be a good time to explore the Abbey, Church and Visitor Centre.

THE ABBEY The original Abbey, built
on the headland, was probably of wood and housed both nuns and monks. It was set up by the Abbess Hilda in 657AD. It was here that Caedmon, a young, shy farm worker became a poet and writer of songs. He is now considered the father of English church music. One night, whilst he was asleep in the stable with the animals, he had a vision calling on him to sing the beginning of created things. His retiring disposition deserted him and he
sang about the creation of the world and the origin of man. He sang about the last judgement and the pains of hell comparing it with the delights of heaven. In AD870 the Abbey was destroyed by Danish raiders, only to be rebuilt again by William de Percy around the 11th century. The magnificent ruin to be seen at Whitby today has suffered badly over the years. A terrible storm in December 1763 felled the western wing, then in June 1830 part of the massive central tower collapsed. In the great storm of January 1839 the wind blew down the south wall Not only did it have to contend with the elements but the German Navy bombarded Whitby in 1914. The front of the Abbey was hit as was the west door. The building is now looked after by English Heritage and is open virtually all year round.

ST. MARY'S CHURCH This is the Parish Church of Whitby and stands on the lofty east cliff, adjacent to the Abbey ruins. Some parts are thought to be older in origin than the Abbey itself but it has undergone lots of alterations in its lifetime. It was renovated and en-larged in 1821, 1822 and 1823 and has a capacity for 2000 worshippers. The tower at the west end contains six excellent bells. In one corner of the burial ground you will find the Caedmon Memorial Cross. It stands twenty feet

high and has some superb carvings and inscriptions on all sides. The inscription reads 'To the glory of God and in memory of Caedmon, the father of English sacred song. Fell asleep hard by, 680.'

THE ROUTE Enough of history, you came here looking for a Fortune and I am sure you will find one, even if it is a little fishy! Walk down the steps past the church (or take the old Donkey road alongside) and keep straight on at the bottom through the old part of Whitby. You will pass some old world shops selling everything from souvenirs to Whitby Jet still made in local workshops and the old market square complete with the historic pillared Market Hall. At the end of the street turn right to the swing bridge. On the left just before the bridge is Grape Lane and the Captain Cook Museum. It is here that the famous explorer James Cook lodged during his ap-prenticeship. Cross the bridge and turn right along side the harbour. As you turn right straight ahead up the hill is Flowergate with the Sutcliffe Gallery, displaying photographs of the days of sail in Whitby by Frank Meadows Sutcliffe. After passing by shops, cafes and fish and chip shops, including the world famous Magpie fish restaurant, you arrive at the fish quay where the days catch is sold and

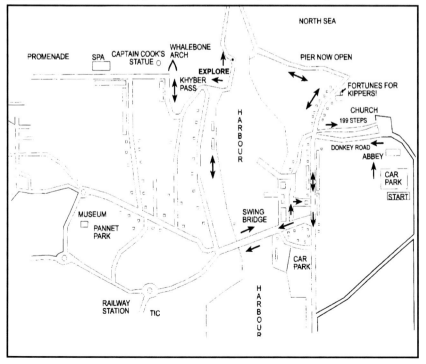

processed, opposite are the amusement arcades, if you wish to try your luck!.
At the end of the amusements is the old lifeboat house and museum. You may now explore the pier and the old lighthouse. Look out for the Khyber Pass road on the left which takes you up to the West Cliff if you wish to visit the Whalebone Arch and Captain Cooks Monument. It is well worth the walk, for the views along the coast and   the panoramic view of Whitby with the Abbey and harbour laid out before you Explore the long pier and the harbour if

Breakwater and lightjhouse

you want to, but now it is time to go in search of the Kipper! Retrace your steps along the fish pier, cross the swing bridge and make your way back to the steps and Donkey road leading to the Abbey.

Do not proceed up the steps or onto the Donkey road but walk along the street on the left, Henrietta Street. Raise your nose into the air and sniff. Follow the smell of smouldering oak and tar mixed with a fishy pong! At the end of the row of houses on the right you will find a Fortune. The old wooden shop and smoke house belonging to the Fortune family is open for the sale of wonderful Kippers. If the smoke house in not in the actual process of smoking ask for a look in, you will be amazed! I will say no more except that you must buy a pair of Kippers, take them home and cook them lightly with care. I will guarantee you will never have eaten a Kipper more tasty, meaty or delicious than a Fortune's oak smoked Kipper. But the pong is another story!

Now that the cliff stabilisation project is complete take a walk past Fortunes and down the steep path onto the pier. This will give you another aspect of Whitby and a different view of the high cliffs. If you look over the wall on the sea side of the pier, you will notice that there is a bypass for the waves to run into. There is the same at the side of the opposite pier. The idea is that when a rough sea is running it pro-tects the harbour allowing the sea to lose some of its force into these channels. Retrace your steps to return up the 99 steps to your car.

The market hall

The Yorkshire Coble is a direct descendant of the Viking longboats. They are designed primarily to work off beaches and are used all along the Yorkshire coast. Today they are mainly used for laying and retrieving lines of crab pots or for tourist rides out to sea. Most now have engines and some a wheelhouse towards the bows. They are locally built and the skills to build and sail these craft have been passed down through the generations. Imagine a larger version of one of these boats crossing the North Sea, it's dragon head prow emerging from the mist to strike terror into the local population possibly even to sack Whitby Abbey.

Cobles in Whitby har-

The Herring

The Herring industry, and thus the Kipper (a smoked herring) is an important part of Whitby's history. As they swarm in huge shoals looking for food, the fishermen had easy pickings. Their nets filled to bursting with wriggling silver bodies as they hauled the shining hoard aboard. The Herring fishery on this coast was of little importance until 1833 when the Whitby Herring Company was formed for the purpose of curing Herrings and other fish for home consumption and export. A curing house was built at Tate Hill. In 1840 the quantity of Herrings taken each season was estimated at 800 lasts (a last, was a measure of the weight of herring caught, being equivalent to about 1000Kilograms today), half of which were purchased by vessels from France & Belgium. Many were sold fresh in the town and about 120 lasts were cured here and at Staithes, Runswick Bay and other small coastal villages. The last remnant of this

Fortun es smokehouse and shop

once thriving industry is Fortune s Kippers which are cured by smoke alone giving them that unique flavour and texture that only an entirely oak smoked Kipper can retain.

Herring caught off the Yorkshire coast start their feeding season in May, further north as plankton becomes plentiful. Through August and September Herring fishing is in full swing as the shoals move south to eventually reach France and Belgium. It was not only local boats that joined in the harvest of the sea, boats from Cornwall also shared in this profitable venture. There was a varying array of boats of different design as they set sail from Scarborough, Whitby, Staithes and other east coast harbours. The fish were gutted on the quay side by Scottish fisher lasses who followed the boats down the coast. Their skill with the knife was legendary. All this work and industry to satisfy our desire for the succulent kipper, caught, gutted, sold, bought and taken to the smoke house to be cured A delicacy that makes my mouth water as I write these words. How did you guess that I love kippers?

ROUTE 4

SMUGGLERS AND BOGGLES
A low tide walk

Smuggling contraband was rife around the coasts of Britain years ago and the people of East Yorkshire were second to none in their efforts to evade the excise man. Robin Hoods Bay hasn't changed much since those tough days. The houses still lean on each other as they cling to the cliff. The sea still pounds against the defences, shaking the foundations of these old houses. Some still have their interconnecting doors and passages through which many a bale of silk or barrel of the finest French Brandy was transported away from suspecting eyes. It is said that it was possible to travel from the sea to the moor using these secret passages without being seen. As you walk around, explore some of the old ginnels and alleys. You will find strange names commemorating something or someone from the past. See if you can find Tommy Baxter Street, The Bolts, Jim Bells Stile and Martin 's Row.

FACT FILE.

Distance -4 miles *(5Y:zkm)*
Time -2 hours
Grading -Easy
Map -OS Landranger 94. OS Outdoor Leisure 27
Start -Car park at Robin Hoods Bay, grid ref. 952052
Refreshments -A good choice of pubs and cafes in Robin Hoods Bay

WARNINGJ This route traverses the sea shore and is not passable with an advancing tide. Please allow at least half an hours brisk walking time on the shore. Take the trouble to check the time of high tide before setting off. Heed this warning as the cliffs are subject to erosion and there is no escape! DO NOT RISK BEING CUT OFF BY THE TIDE!!

THE ROUTE

1.The walk starts from Robin Hoods Bay, a couple of miles   off   the   A171 Scarborough to Whitby road. Park in the old railway station car park in the village and make your way towards the old town, down the very steep hill to the beach, then turn right along the shore.
2.If you take time to explore the sea shore you might find a piece of jet. Jet is the fossilised wood of prehistoric monkey puzzle trees and is worked and polished to make fine jewellery which was so popular with the Victorians. The jet industry was big business in the area around the time of Queen Victoria. Jet is only found on this stretch of the coast.
3.Leave the beach at the first inlet on the right, Boggle Hole. The curious name of Boggle is a Yorkshire name for a Hobgoblin, a mischievous little fellow that used to inhabit these parts! You will see a YHA here. Leave by the road up a steep hill and continue along until the road forks.
4.Take the left fork over a stone bridge crossing the Scarborough to Whitby railway track. Cross the bridge then take the cow path immediately on the right to access the railway track. The track soon crosses a road to scramble up the other side.
5.The track takes you back to the start in a couple of miles. At the road turn right and soon you will come to the car park on your left. Unless you are going to explore the ginnels and alleys and perhaps sample the ale or refreshments in one of the pubs and cafes in Robin Hoods Bay

The Scarborough to Whitby Railway was closed in the Beeching cuts of 1964, leaving Whitby with only one of it's three railway lines This scenic route carried holiday makers and freight between the seaside towns of Scarborough and Whitby. The line from Robin Hoods Bay Station climbed steeply to Ravenscar Station at 600ft.

And a special engine was developed, called the 'Whitby Willie', to cope with the incline. If you listen carefully on a still day you can still hear the engine labouring up the slope, belching steam and smoke as it struggles to pull its coaches crammed full of excited children clutching bucket and spades on their way to Scarborough.

The whole route is now a cycle track and public footpath, giving an endless combination of circular walks if combined with sections of the Cleveland Way which follows the coast (the signposts have acorns on them).

Robin Hoods Bay

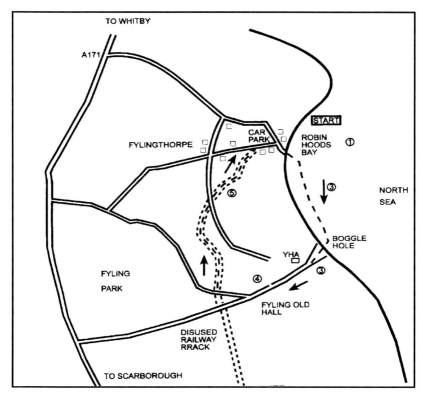

ROUTE 5

BIRDS, SHIPS AND LIGHTHOUSES -A WALK AROUND SPURN HEAD

Spurn head is a nature reserve owned by the Yorkshire Wildlife Trust. It is a resting place for migrating birds attracting bird watchers from all over the country. The headland of Spurn is a continuously shifting spit of land As the erosion of the coast further north provides silt to build a new spit it in turn causes the erosion of the existing peninsula. Each time a new spurn point is built by the sea it is a little further west than the pervious one.

A monastery was built here in 670 and in the late 1200's there was a town, a chapel and even a member of parliament However the sea was obviously not of the same political leaning and washed it away in 1360. Lighthouses have been a feature on the point and more than ten have been built and either washed away or moved as the spit collapsed and then rejuvenated itself. Today's lighthouse was built between 1893 and 1895, but the remains of the pervious one built in 1852 still stands, alas without its lantern which you will find it resting in the mud in the Humber estuary. A few houses remain on the point for the lifeboat crews, Humber lifeboat being one of the most famous in the country. Looking along the Humber estuary to the ships slowly creeping their way into the ports further up the river and the sandbanks all around I think the lifeboat will be needed for some time to come. Unless washed away when the sea reclaims the spit in a winters storm!

FACT FILE

Distance -6 miles (10km)
Time -3 hours walking. Allow more time for exploring.
Grading -Easy
Map -OS Landranger 113
Start -Entrance to Spurn or Spurn car park (fee).
Refreshments -Small cafe run by the lifeboat crew.
When available take the chance to buy a Crab or Lobster on the point. Follow the sign .
displayed.

ROUTE

It is advisable to walk this route when the tide is out. Starting from the Blue Bell Visitor Centre car park follow the Spurn Footpath way markers towards the cliff top. On the way you will pass a sea watching hide and a bird observatory. Follow the path, unless erosion has taken place, when you might have to walk on the road or beach. When approaching the lighthouse the path splits. Go left here where there should be a sign saying 'Seaside path'. This will take you round the headland, on the beach after passing the lighthouse. Once round the headland, the path goes underneath the

The "New" Lighthouse

jetty then to the Spurn car park. Walk in the direction of the sign for Riverside Footpath, Then the Spurn Footpath markers will take you back to the visitor centre. Alternatively you could visit the Yorkshire Wildlife Trust shop then walk back to the road. If you would like to potter and only do the short walk around the head you must park on the Spurn car park. Cross the road and walk over the sand dunes to the beach, then right to walk around the headland and return to the car park under the jetty on the riverside path.

If you would like refreshments the café is past the car park towards the head of the road, but I cannot guarantee it will be open.

Binoculars are a must for this walk to watch the birds and also the regular shipping in and out of the River Humber

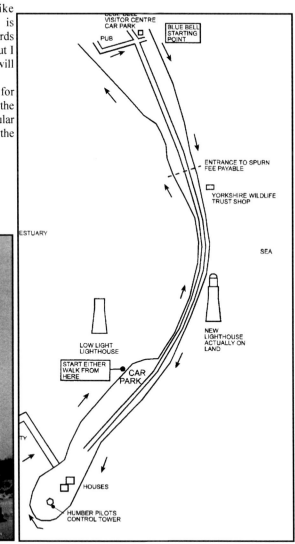

VISITOR CENTRE
CAR PARK

BLUE BELL STARTING POINT

PUB

ENTRANCE TO SPURN
FEE PAYABLE

YORKSHIRE WILDLIFE
TRUST SHOP

ESTUARY

SEA

LOW LIGHT
LIGHTHOUSE

NEW
LIGHTHOUSE
ACTUALLY ON
LAND

START EITHER
WALK FROM
HERE

CAR PARK

HOUSES

HUMBER PILOTS
CONTROL TOWER

The "Old" Lighthouse

ROUTE 6

THE RAVENSCAR ROAM

Ravenscar's heritage includes connections with King George 3rd who used The Hall (then a private house) as a retreat during his bouts of madness. The Hall is now the Raven Hall Hotel and was built in 1774 over the remains of a Roman signal station, one of a chain along the east coast. Alum mining was prominent on this part of the coast in the 17th century. The old workings are being restored and are open for your inspection. There was also a brick company at Ravenscar. The old quarry and remains of the kilns can still be seen along the old railway line towards Robin Hoods Bay. The path leading to the line is paved in places with bricks bearing the Ravenscar Brick company name.

FACT FILE.
Distance -8 miles (13km)
Time -3 hours Grading -Easy
Map -OS Landranger 94
Start -Plenty of roadside parking at Ravenscar Grid Reference -980015

THE ROUTE

Start from the Raven Hall Hotel at Ravenscar and walk back along the road you came on. Continue past the telephone box then turn right at the bridleway sign along Robin Hood Lane. Keep to the track straight ahead when the road expires near the bungalow on the left.

Where the track forks keep straight on. Eventually you will meet the Stoupe Brow road, bear right here and continue downhill all the way to Stoupe Brow Cottage Farm, and enjoy the superb scenery.

Take the sign for the Cleveland Way on the right near the old war relic on the coast and use the cliff path towards Ravenscar. The path winds its way along the cliff top then swerves inland to join a wider path to pass the sign for the Alum Works. The works are worth a look, there are a few ruins and an information board explaining the site.

Follow the yellow arrow through the woods on the right then keep left each time the path forks to return to the Raven Hall Hotel. Walk past the hotel keeping it on your left past the wire fence. Where the fence ends take the Cleveland Way sign to return to the cliff path.

In a little over a mile cross the stile on the right at the public footpath sign across the field to a stone stile. At the road turn right back towards Ravenscar. At the 'T' junction turn right again to take you back to the start and possibly a cup of tea. Me? I think I'll have a

Peak Alum Works.

dip in the hotel swimming pool!
If you visit the alum works look out to sea and try to imagine the flat bottomed ships bringing in their stinking cargo of urine collected from public houses in London and Hull. The urine was mixed with alum shale to help to crystallise it. Most of the land you have walked on belongs to the National Trust. Perhaps you noticed the National Trust Centre at the start of the walk, please give them your support.

Robin Hoods Bay from Ravenscar

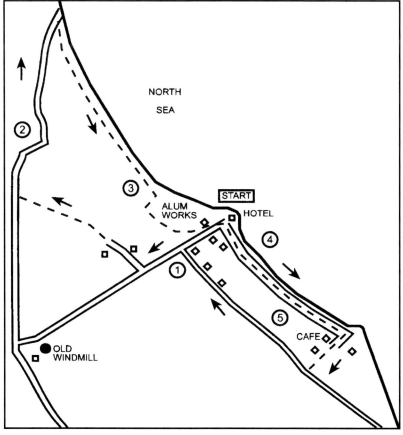

ROUTE 7

THE JUGGER HOWE JOGGLE

The walk over Stoney Marl Moor and Jugger Howe Moor can be exposed in bad weather, go prepared! Jugger Howe was a military training area with connections over the moor to Low North Camp at Harwood Dale. The army had a practice firing range on Jugger Howe after the last war, but the land has now been returned to agriculture and sheep farming.

FACT FILE

Distance -8 miles (13km)
Time -3 hours
Grading -Moderate
Map -OS Landranger 94. OS Outdoor Leisure 27
Start -Ravenscar Grid Reference -980015
Refreshments - take you own

THE ROUTE

This trek begins at Ravenscar perched on the 600ft cliffs high above the North Sea situated between Scarborough and Whitby. There is ample parking as marked on the roadside. Start with the Raven Hall Hotel at your back and walk uphill along the road you arrived on in a westerly direction for about a quarter of a mile. Turn right at the bridleway sign along Robin Hood Lane. Keep straight ahead at the end ofthe road up a rough track following the bridleway sign. Shortly the track forks, take the track to the left and follow the yellow arrow to the road and radio mast.

At the radio mast turn right onto the moor at the bridleway sign opposite. In one mile the track splits, take the bridleway marked with a blue arrow to the right. Follow this to the farm road then turn left still following the sign for the bridleway. After a corner look out on your right for a gate with a blue arrow on it. Turn right here and cross the field diagonally right. Shortly you will reach a gate onto the main road, the busy A171. Cross with care then follow a path across the verge keeping the gorse on your left you soon meet an old road. Go left here then in 100yards go right over a stile into the meadow.

Follow the yellow arrow now keeping close to the line of a fence on your right. Cross a stile bearing right and eventually the path drops down into Wragby Wood to a junction of becks. Follow the path around to the right then when the path splits bear left over a wooden bridge. Follow the path round straight on now following the line of Jugger Howe Beck on your left.